A life in Short Stories

Rose Aiello Morales

Copyright © 2012 Author Name

All rights reserved.

ISBN-10:1481226800
ISBN-13:9781481226806

DEDICATION

I would like to dedicate this book to my husband Alex, who always supported me, to my first publisher, Larry Kuechlin, who had faith in me, and to Mark Paleologo, who always said I could do it.

Thoughts Upon Reading of the State of Man

There is no mother,
never was a father,
we are ripped
from the belly of the beast,
slavering, hungry, born to forage
on whatever scraps the world has left.

We are cursed with sentience,
knowing of the things we do,
fearing nothingness
is all that waits for us,
building dreams to chase away the dark.

The dark remains
festering inside us,
blood-let in each measured drip,
our teeth are sharpened into no point,
no point for those who feel no guilt.

And gilt is painted on our souls lost,
we suffer from purloined redemption,
stuffed unwilling into urns and boxes,
swallowed by the unrelenting Earth.

Ground Zero

Inching toward the time,
another day, hour minute
warm warned and wary,
this may be the coming
of the grate, the only heat
you'll know, one slight slash
of pay stub red away.

A tent of many colors, plastic
tarp surrounds the cardboard
environs and no one knows you down,
out hunkering in season, above
the light will twinkle, smiling Santas,
bells wringing wet, the only pants you own.

And who will see you now?
Is there no manger for a poor soul
searching, straw and the braying
of asses, calling for a trundle
or some floor space waiting,
never any room at the Inn.

Now you see the world,
upside from the ground up,
invisible armies marching
to Salvation, God is watching,
frowning, but our arms are filled

with our own presence, and not
a drop of goodness left for beggars.

Shroud

Years pile upon my face,
the soot and grease
of decades filtering mud.

Slung shroud I wear, sari
imitations, guilt woven
into thin wrapped threads.

A weaver's nightmare unravels,
I am cut of peculiar cloth
the wharf just slightly biased.

I use its folds as towel,
then, sorry at how I cheapened it,
I send it on to Turin for its cleaning.

Jigsaw Universe

The pieces are there,
scattered on tables
out of the way, corners,
sides, a touch of sky, grass,
polished wood boundaries
waiting for unification.

I am the drop on the floor,
the rough cut jig, saw flush at my throat,
I cannot move but dream life away.

Flat universe, the void curves
around me and I undulate,
searching shape and form,
a postulate unproven, watching
from the security of empty space.

Expand, contract, I am the bang
and the whimper, ice and fire
at the point of impact, slow moves,
slow morph, I am the evolution
of the worried mind released.

Twitch and stretch, I am the die cut
model no one copies, I find a place
to fit, in place the picture coalesces,
others jump from edges, table discussions,
we are joined for but a nano, then we disappear.

Rhapsody On A Theme of Paganini

Somewhere I've never been
but long to be, taken by a single
key, in time I close my eyes
to water falling, drifts of icy melt
of seasons, spring in bud goes
on and on, the open petals
of a rose inviting, the ears
do runs and heart follows, leaping
scales of green and purple flash.

I see the music in a droplet,
another gathers in a clef-ted

bosom, love beyond the years,
I swell through octave's phrases,
a rhapsody of trills, the thrumming
of the strings and then a pause, I sigh.

The end is the beginning as it starts again.

Dive

Situational clouds beckon,
I count nine and nine and nine
and never get the dim sum twice.

I swim in special sauce,
water wings fried in peanut oil,

you never know until you taste it.

Observe the body never beautiful,
an advocate of demand and conquer,
mind over anything that matters.

Mind you, something never messed
or dirty, my smarts are rolling in the street
when sweepers come, the morning clean immaculate.

The battle scars of arms lifted, stance
so melded to the ground, my burnt skin
shines in rough dive, mind immersed in real.

Ticks

Sleep counts
in the moments

before numb night,
writing slights as ticks
on the wall, sheep offenders
jumping fences, ready for the slaughter.

The moon is a grindstone,
it sharpens nails to talons,
teeth to vampire points,
the tongue is split rapier,
a lover's tease before the venom.

The good show too,
pieces of the pure red beat
roped off, presence in the morning
while the Sun shines shyly
for the newly wakened, nudging in decision.

Let the organ call the supplicants
who open eyes, anticipating
raise or lower, the laying on
of stones and how the scales will tip

Only the coffee knows.

Stick

She held religion like a stick
a cup of poison in her hand

and spoke in tongues forked,
crawling on her belly spewing dogma.

Three legs were chewed,
chained to Eden's shackles.
Christ, that it should come to this,
a witness tainted from the act of seeing.

Her eyes were almond pupils,
a cat that tortures mice
while teasing with the cheese,
the goat's milk rancid in the finding.

Rigid in the stance,
she stood spread eagle
in the water, drowning supplicants,
their sacrifice made rivers red.

She crawled upon the belly of the beast,
her forked tongue lapping at the scarlet robe.
Cardinal, the poison in her gilded cup,
she drank, and stirred religion with a stick.

Enigma

I shall teach you
letters and symbols,
how the eye watches
at all times and turns
its way away, looking,
at things none of us will find.

I is a letter you think you know,
but never see, hidden under layers,
in the leaf etched margins of books,
not meant to reveal at first glance,
the leather cover wears gilt with age.

I shall teach you to read,
all that is written cannot be spoke,
cannot be grasped with hand/eye,
this is not a contest of the flowery,
snipping hedges into pretty shapes,
the blind man is amazed but finds his way.

There are lines beside the linear,
see from the center out, not this
and this and this, but 'A', and 'X'
'Q' divided, forms fall in tangents,
pink comes red again, again we find
the difference, wine decanted many times
gives nuance to its color and roseate feathers grow.

Bite the Bullet

Trash waiting,
the truck comes every year
depositing failure,
we burn it as fuel,
a raging fire keeps us warm.

Scribbled laments,
the epic of a lifetime
swimming in it, stashed
behind pulp fiction and no one
knows just what to name it.

Pejoratives in boxes,
love in rejection, cross
the bad to a short sentence,
prison seems like heaven mixed,
parole a long grasp out of reach.

Wallpaper in the hall
reminds us, critics only reach
the foyer, they show treatises
expounding on the word no.
We kick the door, missing. They limp out.

Mark writes paeans to John
while his wife saves cartons,
vinyl testaments, a claim to fame.

Lennon with a bullet, like all of us
who live in irony, shot to #1 seconds after death.

Gordian

There are no points to this
nor any short way there.
What you see are diamonds
in the rough, tenuous, we call them 'A'.

Death imagined on the other side,
a membrane made of gauze
we float through, searching
for a better term, we call it 'B'.

Distance is a line, not.
Curved space rotates,
ideas are challenged
and we find what's real is knot.

Universe and universe,
they talk and talk and words
lose meaning, angry is the juice
that ties intestinal in knots.

Fingers feel the pinch, we spin

and spin a story into cloth, add
characters and clauses, beginning
is the end, the end is the beginning,
our minds unraveling the secret knot.

Skin Deep

Wound,
fast heal antiseptic,
plastic and band aids.

Box of tissues scar,
I dust tracks lightly,
a history of bloodshed.

Swallow sleep,
dreams remind me,
slights relived as visions.

I drink rancor, my morning coffee,
shrugs and sweaters hold in cold,
hot breath in silver tears of snow.

There's beauty
in complete collapse,
far beyond the skin deep.

Puritanical

Sub vocal greetings
in the Puritan morn,
we tip invisible hats to invisible smiles.

Staunch, twisted in the pot,
starch boiled all day long
and not a thing to chew upon.

What passes for an upward turn,
quick glance, red tail tucked, securely hidden,

the black clad compose their letters.

Sub vocal once again,
we hear in radar, code crack of dawn,
the things they mean but never meant to say.

Funk

Wired,
you wrap it around you,
make love to dis consolation,
swallow the worm

still surviving on dregs
gathered at the bottom.

Water has no meaning,
you weep for emphasis,
all is mud, the source of wallow,
it will never wash you clean.

I squat, searching for a spot
less forlorn, it lives under branches
of a dying tree, the tree hangs on, believing.

Shall I offer up myself? A worthy bargain,
down upon my knees, a beggar's
supplication, a bridge between the sagas.

Instead I stand, look, walk away,
the only option left for one inoculated once.

Bird

For Lisa G.

We are not
the kind who gather,
magpies in the early morn,
news travels fast as nonsense.

Here we sit
at far ends of the wire,
whole notes as emphasis,
apropos of nothing of import.

The world consists
of fractals, fractions,
we are not a one note bird,
our songs cut up for mass consumption.

Are there ever
too many notes?
For love, for joy,
for nothing more
or less than being?

Sing your song, lone bird,
and I'll sing mine, for in the end
we sing for no one but ourselves.

Castaway

Cast, cast away,
the red mark
against a flawless face.

Cast aside,
Cast aground,
your usefulness is gone.

Cling to sharpened hooks,
hooks fashioned, steel claws
withdrawn, no fish are caught this time.

I have no need
for piscatorial fantasies,
I put aside rent cloth, grief cast aside.

The hair shirt does not fit,
I turn it inside out,
its warmth surrounds me.

Perched above the churn
and drag, all cast away,
filament as net, my bounty overflows.

A Life of Small Stories

We make them up,
perhaps before they're due,
living up, down, to expectations,
our lives made up of small decisions.

Pen pauses at junctions,
the wind blows crazy, beautiful
at crossroads, services and services of forks,
knives, pablum spooned in willing mouths
and it tastes like Heaven's manna.

Change protagonists, an action swirls
in villain's eyes, we act all parts, write
all death's conclusions, pages tossed
to cyclones, in the deluge we can pick,
and choose, and sometimes have it chosen.

Anticlimax, life's cessation, a tale told
by madmen, told to antecedents, those
who supervene, the left are tasked
in tiny doses, making sense for senseless.

Far From the Tree

Tree diseased at the elm,
twisted in binds that tie,
imprisoned in the withered bosom,
strangled in the fallow earth,
raised in dirt and shat upon.

Tender flower weakened
at the bud, her fragrance
overcomes, the skin a rosy hue,
strange fruit survives a brutal harvest,
the sweetest apple ripens with the hardest core.

Souls in the Absence of Motion

For women the best aphrodisiacs are words. The G-spot is in the ears. He who looks for it below there is wasting his time. -Isabel Allende

My soul is not in there.

No deep may touch it there,
No romance words
nor love's entreaties,
there is no outlet of attachment.

A moment mastered

beyond mind's touch,
electric fingers pulsing neurons,
expressions waxing, waning
in the false of moonlit night.

My soul is not in there

It whispers in before
and after, punctuated
words, the closeness
of a shared idea forever.

Transcending body's signals,
massed humanity of tissue,
fluid motion in a timeless dance,
the music ends, the spell is broken,
morphing into nothing, everything.
Once in a lifetime you may find

my soul is not in there.

Winter White

Remember
the feel of leaves
the steady crunch
denoting change, I held
my breath, hands at sides

forestalling time, no movement,
sound to spoil timeless moments.

Remember
arms, legs, joy exploding in a signal
as the heights beckoned,
the valley undulated slow,
as if the seasons stood stilled, until
we chose a path and left leaves falling.

Eyes like Nikon magic,
lithe lash glowed like powder
shimmer on a reddened cheek
turned orange, gold, a thousand
myriad pixels flowed in puzzles, then
refocused on the only face that ever mattered.

Tree fall smashed against the sodden Earth
until made hard by fast freeze, white out, your walk
disappeared from view, replaced by icy stares of Winter.

~

Remember
Solstice of December
when the night was long as day,
softened by a touch of snow,
the gentle pale of all things ending
in a fall of lip, then rising, smiling sadly.

CONTENTS

ABOUT THE AUTHOR

Rose Aiello Morales is a poet living in Miami, Fl. She has lived in many different places though, and writes with a knowledge of these places. She had her first poem published at the age of seven. She wrote through high school and through her studies at Rutgers University, then life caught up with her and she stopped for about 20 years. The advent of social networks made her want to try once more, and so she has, for seven years writing continuously.

Made in the USA
San Bernardino, CA
22 April 2013